# A man just like us

## ELIJAH

by Liam Goligher

**thegoodbook**
COMPANY

A man just like us
The good book guide to Elijah
© Liam Goligher/The Good Book Company, 2014.
Series Consultants: Tim Chester, Tim Thornborough,
                    Anne Woodcock, Carl Laferton

The Good Book Company
Tel (UK): 0333 123 0880
Tel (US): 866 244 2165
Tel (int): + (44) 208 942 0880
Email: info@thegoodbook.co.uk

**Websites**
**UK:** www.thegoodbook.co.uk
**North America:** www.thegoodbook.com
**Australia:** www.thegoodbook.com.au
**New Zealand:** www.thegoodbook.co.nz

ISBN: 9781909559240

Printed in the Czech Republic

# CONTENTS

# introduction: good book guides

Every Bible-study group is different—yours may take place in a church building, in a home or in a cafe, on a train, over a leisurely mid-morning coffee or squashed into a 30-minute lunch break. Your group may include new Christians, mature Christians, non-Christians, mums and tots, students, businessmen or teens. That's why we've designed these *Good Book Guides* to be flexible for use in many different situations.

Our aim in each session is to uncover the meaning of a passage, and see how it fits into the "big picture" of the Bible. But that can never be the end. We also need to appropriately apply what we have discovered to our lives. Let's take a look at what is included:

⊕ **Talkabout:** Most groups need to "break the ice" at the beginning of a session, and here's the question that will do that. It's designed to get people talking around a subject that will be covered in the course of the Bible study.

⊥ **Investigate:** The Bible text for each session is broken up into manageable chunks, with questions that aim to help you understand what the passage is about. **The Leader's Guide** contains **guidance on questions**, and sometimes ☺ additional "follow-up" questions.

☺ **Explore more (optional):** These questions will help you connect what you have learned to other parts of the Bible, so you can begin to fit it all together like a jig-saw; or occasionally look at a part of the passage that's not dealt with in detail in the main study.

⊖ **Apply:** As you go through a Bible study, you'll keep coming across **apply** sections. These are questions to get the group discussing what the Bible teaching means in practice for you and your church. ☺ **Getting personal** is an opportunity for you to think, plan and pray about the changes that you personally may need to make as a result of what you have learned.

⊕ **Pray:** We want to encourage prayer that is rooted in God's word—in line with his concerns, purposes and promises. So each session ends with an opportunity to review the truths and challenges highlighted by the Bible study, and turn them into prayers of request and thanksgiving.

The **Leader's Guide** and introduction provide historical background information, explanations of the Bible texts for each session, ideas for **optional extra** activities, and guidance on how best to help people uncover the truths of God's word.

# why study Elijah?

Elijah stands out in the Bible as one of God's all-time greats. He's right up there alongside Moses, as one of the duo who appeared alongside Jesus on the Mount of Transfiguration. Elijah blasted into the national life of Israel like a tornado, sweeping through the land until eventually he was caught up into heaven in a whirlwind.

Elijah served the one true God at an epic time in the history of Israel. In the ninth century BC, God's Old Testament people—the nation of Israel—were deeply mired in idolatry and apostasy. God worked through Elijah and his heir, Elisha, in a succession of miracles not seen since the days of Moses and not to be seen again until the time of Jesus.

Israel could never forget Elijah, so great was the impact. They kept saying: *He'll be back!* And Jesus himself pointed to John the Baptist as the returned Elijah, whose arrival in Israel signalled the imminent appearance of the long-awaited Messiah.

Yet the New Testament writer James describes Elijah as *a man just like us*. Elijah wasn't infallible or perfect. His life displays the kind of humanity for which you and I are noted—marked by weakness, failure, frustration and anxiety. It was through this one man—someone just like us—that God magnificently confronted and exposed the false religion Israel had been seduced by, and the murderous corruption that went with it.

In our day, too, most people imagine that God is irrelevant to their lives, and look to other "gods" for what they need. These pressures affect Christians as well. We are often few in number and feel insignificant. Like Elijah, we may even suspect that God has abandoned us.

But through God's grace Elijah persevered. Ultimately his life and ministry revealed God's sovereignty, grace, provision, resurrection power, inescapable justice and his awesome salvation. How much could we learn from Elijah for ourselves, in our situations today? The true story of Elijah gives us a great opportunity to discover how God can take people just like us to use for his eternal glory.

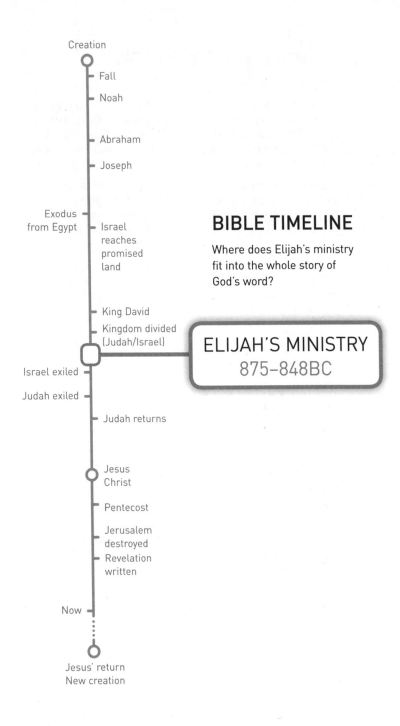

Creation

Fall

Noah

Abraham

Joseph

Exodus from Egypt

Israel reaches promised land

## BIBLE TIMELINE

Where does Elijah's ministry fit into the whole story of God's word?

King David

Kingdom divided (Judah/Israel)

## ELIJAH'S MINISTRY
### 875–848BC

Israel exiled

Judah exiled

Judah returns

Jesus Christ

Pentecost

Jerusalem destroyed

Revelation written

Now

Jesus' return
New creation

# 1

## 1 Kings 16 v 29 – 17 v 24
# BOOT CAMP

## ⊕ talkabout

1. In what ways do people today think that our modern world has made progress, compared with previous generations?

   *Science, technology, education.*

   • What do people who think like this often believe about "the idea of God"?

   *Insignificant, myth.*

## ⊙ investigate

Elijah appears in the Old Testament about 900 years before Christ. Ancient Israel has been divided into two kingdoms, and King Ahab is ruler of the larger northern kingdom.

▶ **Read 1 Kings 16 v 29 – 17 v 1**

2. During his reign, Ahab fortified a number of his cities, formed profitable trade agreements with surrounding nations, and had some success in military campaigns. What aspect of Ahab's reign is highlighted in chapter 16?

   *married Jezebel.*
   *Temple to Baal.*

> **DICTIONARY**
>
> **Judah (16 v 29):** the southern kingdom after Israel was divided (see timeline, p6).
> **Samaria (v 29):** the capital of the northern kingdom of Israel.
> **Jeroboam (v 31):** first king of the northern kingdom, who was remembered as evil.
> **Sidonians (v 31):** people from the pagan city of Sidon, in Phoenicia, north of Israel.
> **Baal, Asherah (v 32, 33):** false gods.

• Why only this, do you think?

*No other gods before me.*
*Heathen marriages forbidden.*
*Ex. 20:3.*

The false god Baal was associated with weather and fertility. Baal-worshippers believed that if they appeased him, typically through cult prostitution, he would send good weather and their crops would flourish.

3. Elijah brings Ahab a message from the "LORD" (God's name as revealed in his covenant with Israel). As he speaks, what do we learn about…
• Elijah's convictions about God?

*1 4 v 1. God lives - present.*
*God more important than Ahab.*

• Elijah's understanding about himself?

*God's servant, at His disposal.*

**Note:** Literally, Elijah says: "As the LORD, the God of Israel, lives, before whom I stand…"

4. Imagine what it would be like to stand in front of Ahab and announce this unwelcome news from the God that he so openly provoked and disobeyed. How could Elijah be so bold?

*The Lord God of Israel,*
*all powerful.*

• **Read Deuteronomy 11 v 16-17.** By what authority could Elijah speak to Ahab like this?

*God's word - drought if they*
*sinned against Him*

- When Elijah promises the Baal-worshipping King Ahab that there will be no rain, what spiritual contest does he announce?

*Baal versus God of Israel Draught.*

"The word of the LORD came to X": this is how the Old Testament usually introduces a new prophet. But not Elijah: so some think that at this point Elijah was not yet called to be a prophet. However, he surely acts like one.

5. **Read James 5 v 17.** What insight does this give us into Elijah's faith and passion?

*He believed God's Word. and wanted people to keep God's honour.*

→ **apply**

6. What is needed for Christians today to be more like Elijah? Think about:
   • what he confidently knew about God.

*Convinced of God's sovereignty*

   • how he viewed himself.

*Available to be led by God.*

   • what he prayed for (James 5 v 17).

*God's will to be done.*

Elijah spoke into an age like ours. Just as Israel practised idolatry, people today turn to all sorts of spiritual beliefs and lifestyles that seem "broad-minded". By contrast, Elijah had one overriding conviction: the invisible Lord lives, and we cannot avoid or escape him. Is that your conviction?

How has your confidence in the presence of the living God sometimes been undermined by the "modern" ideas of our age?

How will you resist the influence of these wrong ideas?

⊙ **investigate**

❯ **Read 1 Kings 17 v 2-24**

**7.** Look at verse 3. What is surprising about God's instruction to Elijah?

*He is told to go & hide.*

**8.** What do you think Elijah learns about God in the Kerith Ravine?

*He can provide for us anywhere and in any way.*

• What would he learn when the brook dried up?

*God had more plans for Elijah he had to move on. Widow came to know god of Israel although a Gentile.*

Significantly, God sends Elijah next to the region of Sidon, the homeland of Jezebel, who is known for her devotion to Baal and promoting Baal idolatry in Israel (see 1 Kings 16 v 31 and 18 v 19).

**9.** What has been the effect in Sidon of God's word spoken by Elijah in Israel?

*Drought in Sidon.*

**10.** What does God reveal about himself in Sidon, by providing food for Elijah, the widow and her son?

*He is alive.*

• What does God reveal about himself by raising the widow's son to life again?

*Miracle working God giver of life.*

**11.** How does the living God compare with Baal?

*Baal cannot defend the people – man made.*

---

(:) **explore more**

optional

Jesus referred to this story when he was teaching in Nazareth.

▶ **Read Luke 4 v 16-30**

*What are the similarities between Israel in Elijah's day and Nazareth in Jesus' day?* *Refused God's Word.*

*What response from God to Israel's rebellion in the time of Elijah does Jesus highlight here?* *Widow – Gentile – miracles*

*In Luke 4, what is Jesus saying about himself and the gospel that would be preached in his name?* *Gentiles would respond to the gospel*

**Read Acts 13 v 44-48** to see one instance of how this came true.

*Paul turns to Gentiles.*

## ➡ apply

**12.** Think about the experience of Elijah, when God took him out of the limelight and sent him far away into the wilds. What can we learn through such experiences about...
- God's priority for our lives? – *to know Him better.*
- God's provision? *Not to presume, never forgotten*
- God's purposes—in what he does and doesn't give us?

*Knows what is best · plans for us in love. Well know the reason one day. He is sovereign.*

---

## ⋯ getting personal

Sometimes in life the brook Kerith dries up. Our health suddenly deteriorates, our job comes to an end, our relationships break down, or our fruitful ministry disappears.

When things in your life suddenly go pear-shaped, what can you expect God still to be doing? *& still loves us.*

How will that change your perspective on life in that moment (perhaps that's now)?
*Trust Him more.*

## ⬆ pray

**Praise and thank the LORD...** who lives, who speaks to this world, who acts with sovereign power, who provides for our needs, and who shows grace to the undeserving.

**Confess times...** when you have feared other people more than the LORD.

**Ask God...** to help you fear, hear, obey, serve and trust him, as Elijah did.

# 2 1 Kings 18 v 1-39
# STANDING ALONE

*The story so far*

Elijah shows us how to fear and serve the living LORD, and him alone; he boldly spoke God's word, followed his instructions, and revealed his power and grace.

## ⊕ talkabout

1. Share examples of situations in which you have had to stand alone as a Christian. What helped you to stand firm? What was the outcome?

## ⊕ investigate

❯ **Read 1 Kings 18 v 1-2 and 15-21**

2. Why did God choose a drought to show his anger against Israel's worship of Baal, do you think? (Hint: Check out note about Baal on page 8.)

> **DICTIONARY**
>
> **Obadiah (v 16):** Ahab's palace administrator, who met Elijah while on an errand for his master.

*Deut. 11 : 16, 17.*
*God's warning to Israel.*

• What was the consequence of God's action for his prophet (v 17)?

*Elijah blamed for drought.*

**3.** How complete was Israel's rejection of the LORD (v 21)?

*Tried to serve both God & Baal.*

**4.** What did Elijah challenge them to do?

*To choose.*

• What was the big thing he wanted them to understand about God?

*Can't mix truth & error.*

## → apply

**5.** Like Israel in Elijah's time, many people today try to mix Christian teaching with ideas from other beliefs, thinking this enriches Christianity and makes Christians broad-minded. Can you think of any examples of this?

*Appease other faiths.*

• Which ideas is it most tempting to combine with Christian teaching in your culture and community?

*Only faith in finished work of Jesus will take us to Heaven. no merits of our own.*

## ⊡ getting personal

What people today call broad-mindedness, the Bible calls double-mindedness.

If Elijah were a prophet today, would he have good reason to ask you: "How long will you waver between two opinions?"

What is most likely to divide your heart and mind, so that you no longer follow the LORD God alone?

Read and heed Jesus' warning to his disciples in **Matthew 6 v 24**.

## ⬇ investigate

> **Read 1 Kings 18 v 22-39**

The story of Elijah on Mount Carmel is one of the great set-piece dramas in Bible history, teaching one of the greatest lessons about God. Mount Carmel is a coastal mountain area; up to 546m (1810ft) high, it extends south-east from modern-day Haifa.

6.  How did the prophets of Baal try to get the atttention of their god?
    • v 26 (3 things mentioned)

    *Prepared a sacrifice*
    *called on him; the altar.*
    *Danced around the altar.*
    • v 28 *Cut themselves.*

7.  What was their strategy, do you think?

    *No relationship - ~~man made~~*
    *~~by~~ ~~a~~, wanted a show*
    *of power - Satan's power.*

    • What does this show us about their view of Baal and the kind of relationship they had with him?

    *Not a person.*

**8.** How did Elijah respond to the Baal-worshippers' attempts to persuade their god to produce fire? What was he showing Israel?

*Mocked them.*

**9.** What did Elijah do?
- v 30 *Repaired the altar.*

- v 31 *Took 12 stones rep. tribes of Israel. Dug a trench, filled it with water.*
- v 32-35 *Prepared wood & sacrifice - he drenched it with water three times.*

- v 36-37 *Time of evening sacrifice - for sins. He prays.*

- Why did Elijah focus this contest on offering a sacrifice, do you think? (Compare Leviticus 1 v 3-9.)

*Shedding of blood only covering for sin in O.T. ritual.*

**10.** What does this event show us about what God is like?

*Answers prayers of His people if they are obedient - all powerful.*

• What does it show us about Elijah's relationship with God?

*Trusts God to answer as witness to Israel.*

## explore more

optional

Elijah staged this showdown to demonstrate that God is the only true God, and that all other gods are mere pretenders. But this spectacular event was only a preview of a far greater display that was to come.

Read the words of John the Baptist about Jesus in **John 1 v 29** and **Matthew 3 v 11-12**. See also **Acts 2 v 1-4**.
*How do both the sacrifice and the fire on Mount Carmel preview Jesus Christ?*

God showed that he accepted the sacrifice that Elijah offered by answering his prayer and sending fire. And God sent the "fire" of the Holy Spirit (Acts 2 v 3-4) to show that he accepted Christ's sacrifice (Acts 2 v 32-33).

The fire on Mount Carmel marked the ending of the drought in Israel (1 Kings 18 v 41-45).

▶ **Read Acts 2 v 36-41**

*What did the Spirit's coming mark for God's people at Pentecost?*

## apply

11. The prophets of Baal approached their god by engaging in "magic"—formulas or behaviours that try to influence the god to do what you want. How can we fall into the same mistake in approaching God?

*No experience of conversion nominal adherents*

• What are the tell-tale signs of the "magic" approach to God?

*Outward expression but no spiritual experience*

**12.** Elijah approached the Lord on the basis of a sacrifice for sin and by faith. What does this look like for Christians today?

*Come to the Father through work of the Cross by the Son.*

• What are the tell-tale signs of this?

*Assurance of Salvation. Come by Grace through faith. no merit of our own.*

## ↑ pray

God has given people such proofs of his existence—such demonstrations of his power, such displays of his character, such a revelation of his will—that all our unbelief and all our refusal to give him his rightful place in our lives is utterly inexcusable. But… he will not force himself upon us. He offers himself for our acceptance. Don't hop between two opinions. If the Lord is God, then follow him.

**Thank God…**

**Confess to God…**

**Ask God…**

# 3 1 Kings 19
# FEELING DOWN

## The story so far

Elijah shows us how to fear and serve the living LORD, and him alone; he boldly spoke God's word, followed his instructions, and revealed his power and grace.

The LORD is the only God: we cannot serve him alongside anything else, or manipulate him by anything we do, or approach him without a sacrifice for sin.

## ⊕ talkabout

1. Can you think of a time in your life when a high point was followed by a low point? How did it affect you?

## ⊥ investigate

> **Read 1 Kings 18 v 36-46**

2. Summarise all the things that would have made this point in Elijah's life the pinnacle of his ministry so far.

> **DICTIONARY**
>
> **Jezreel (v 46):** city in northern Israel, where Ahab had his palace.

*People acknowledged God was Lord*
*Prophets of Baal killed.*
*Rain fell - drought finished*
*Empowered to run before Ahab.*

• What might he expect to happen next, do you think?

*Spiritual revival.*

> **Read 1 Kings 19 v 1-9**

3. What happens to Elijah next, and how does he respond?

*Threatened by Jezebel.*
*Runs for his life to Beersheba.*

• In what way are his expectations disappointed, do you think?

*No one supports him.*

4. What details reveal his state of mind?

*v 3. Sends his servant away.*
*v 4. wanted to die.*
*v 5. wearied, slept. (?)*

5. What are the first actions that God took (v 5b-9) to help his prophet overcome this depressed feeling?

*Sent an angel. (Lord)*
*Gave him sleep.*
*Fed him.*

• What does this show us about God's care for his people?

*Helps & provides for all our needs, mental & physical*

## ⚃ explore more

> **❯ Read Exodus 3 v 1-15; 33 v 6 and 18-22**

*What is significant about the place where Elijah ended up?*

*mt. of god. moses.*

## ⤷ apply

**6.** What can we learn here about godly ways to approach fellow Christians who are feeling low?

*Not always spiritual. alone.*
*Be a friend - lonely people.*
*Emphasise God's love & care for*
*each one.*

## ⌂ getting personal

We underestimate the resilient power of evil—the way it comes back again, and again, and again. When Elijah won the contest with the prophets of Baal, he must have thought: "Job done!" Baal was humiliated; the enemy was defeated. He'd heard the people say: "The LORD—he is God". Surely they'd been converted... Surely the battle had been won... But not so!

You think you've overcome sin in one area of your life, but then it appears somewhere else. The reality is that sin is resilient—it's going to be with us all the way to heaven. Where in your life at the moment is evil proving to be resilient?

> **❯ Read Ephesians 6 v 10-18**

What will help you respond to the resilient power of sin and evil? *The love & power of god - His promises*

## ⤓ investigate

> **❯ Read 1 Kings 19 v 9-21**

**7.** Why does God ask Elijah the question in verses 9 and 13, do you think?

*make Elijah think why he had run away.*

- What does Elijah's answer (v 10 and 14) reveal about his thinking?

*Blamed God for his situation.*

**8.** In what way does God choose to reveal his presence to Elijah? And what ways does he not choose?

*Still small voice, spoke to him. Not the earthquake or fire.*

- What is Elijah being taught?

*Word of God most important*

**9.** How does God deal with Elijah's perceived isolation?

*Puts him to work, gives him a companion.*

**10.** What is God's plan for Elijah from this point on?

*No retirement – Elisha to be his successor.*

## ➔ apply

**11.** What can we learn from God's actions about how we further help Christians who are feeling low? Think about the place of the following things:

- God's word — *All important - use against Satan - power of God.*

- God's people — *We all need fellowship, neglect not - - - x HEB. 10:25.*

- God's work — *By Helping each other we help ourselves. Always someone worse off than ourselves.*

**12.** What has been your attitude to God's word, God's people and God's work when you have felt down and discouraged?

*Tell the Lord how we feel and ask for his help and grace.*

- What should (and can) your attitude be?

*Do what the Lord tells us to do.*

## ⊡ getting personal

When God deals with people, he speaks to them. God is speaking to you through his word now. It can change your whole life. It may be the most supernatural thing that you ever experience.

In the low points of our lives, God calls us to listen to his words, trust his promises and worship him. How does that challenge the attitudes that we often slip into at these times? And how should it also comfort us?

## ⊡ explore more

*optional*

Jesus suffered the most extreme anguish in Gethsemane (Luke 22 v 39-46). But Jesus was no comic-book superhuman: temptation, hatred, betrayal, pain, injustice, humiliation, abandonment and the experience of God's wrath aginst sin ("this cup", v 42) didn't simply bounce harmlessly off him.

▶ **Read Hebrews 2 v 14-18**

*What practical help for us has been provided through Christ's anguish and suffering (Hebrews 4 v 15-16)?*

*He knows, loves, cares, understands & sympasises.*

## ⬆ pray

**Praise and thank God...**

for his tender compassion towards us, in our weakness, struggles and failures; and for Jesus Christ, who suffered and who sympathises with us in all that we suffer.

**Confess times...**

when you have feared other people more than God, when you have wallowed in self-pity, and when you have given up on his word, his people and his work.

**Ask God...**

to help you show godly love and support that is practical and spiritual, tender and robust, to people you know who are suffering as Elijah did.

# **4** 1 Kings 21
# CONFRONTING INJUSTICE

*The story so far*

Elijah shows us how to fear and serve the living Lord, and him alone; he boldly spoke God's word, followed his instructions, and revealed his power and grace.

The LORD is the only God: we cannot serve him alongside anything else, or manipulate him by anything we do, or approach him without a sacrifice for sin.

As God helped Elijah, so we should help people who feel low, both practically and spiritually, pointing them to God's word, people and work, and to Christ.

## ⊕ **talkabout**

**1.** Describe a time when you knew it was right to tell someone something difficult. What excuses came to mind to justify putting off or avoiding this difficult conversation?

• If you did go through with it, what helped you to do that?

## ⊤ **investigate**

▶ **Read 1 Kings 21 v 1-6**

**2.** How does King Ahab's request (v 2) sound reasonable?

> Better vineyard or money.

Before the people of Israel entered the promised land, Moses was told by the LORD himself to use lots to divide the land between the various tribal groups in Israel (Numbers 26 v 52-56). Family groups would receive land based on who their ancestors were. Moses never entered the land, so the allocation was finally carried out by Joshua, following the LORD's instructions to Moses (Joshua 11 v 23).

**3.** **Read Leviticus 25 v 23 and Numbers 36 v 7.** What do we learn from God's law about how the Israelites were to treat the land?

> Not to be sold permanently the land is God's land. Each tribe keep their inheritance

• **Read Deuteronomy 17 v 18-20.** What was expected of the kings of Israel? What, then, would have been expected of King Ahab in this situation?

> Write out the law and ~~not to be sold~~ keep it. - forbidden to buy Naboth's vineyard - it was his inheritance for him and his descendants.

**4.** Why could Ahab's offer have seemed tempting to Naboth?

> Better vineyard.
> Please the king.

**5.** How would you describe Ahab's state of mind over his plans for a vegetable garden?

> Covetness become an obsession. Acted like a spoilt child.

**6.** Why does Naboth refuse Ahab's offer?

*Forbidden by the Law to sell his inheritance.*

• What motivates him to turn down Ahab, do you think?

*Please God & obey him before the king.*

## ⤷ apply

**7.** Today, how might Christians have to choose between obeying God, or disobeying him in order to get on in the world? Think about the following areas:

• the governing authorities

*To avoid prison or death. Protect their families*

• the workplace

*Cheating or covering up. Gossip or bad language.*

• the local community

*minorities. all religions uniting.*

• friends and family

*Lord first even above friends & family. Controversial issues.*

## ⇥ apply

**8.** **Read Acts 4 v 18-31.** What do Peter and John teach Christians about how to respond to pressure to disobey God from those in authority?

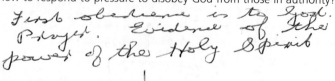

*First obedience is to God. Prayer. Evidence of the power of the Holy Spirit*

- What do these first Christians teach us about where to find the strength and boldness to do that? ⬇

## ⊡ getting personal

Every day we face some sort of choice like the one Naboth faced. Will we cave in to "people pressure", or will we obey God? It may mean:
- refusing to cosy up to big people
- opting out of joining the in-crowd
- being content that some think we're weird because we live differently as God's people
- being resented because we stand between people and their desires
- suffering gossip, slander, false accusations, relationship breakdown or worse—even job loss, legal action or physical harm.

How will you prepare yourself ahead of time for situations like these?

## ⬇ investigate

### ❯ Read 1 Kings 21 v 5-16

**9.** How would you describe Jezebel's view of kingship?

*Ahab above God – absolute rule*

## explore more

▶ **Read Isaiah 32 v 1-8**

Here is God's view of what a king and his kingdom should (and should not) be like.
*At what points did Ahab's kingship and kingdom depart from this?*
*How is all this fulfilled in the kingdom of Christ?*

*Turned away from God to idols.*

▶ **Read 1 Kings 21 v 17-29**

**10.** What message for Ahab did God give Elijah at the end of this story?

• What was Ahab's attitude to Elijah (v 20), and what does it show?

**11.** Look at the timing of the LORD's word to Ahab (v 16-18). Why did God wait until this point, do you think?

• What do you think Ahab's response to God's message shows (v 27-29)— that he was repentant or not? Why? (Skim-reading 22 v 1-28 may help.)

## ⮕ apply

**12.** Why is it so important today that Christians continue to teach people about God's judgment?

• Why do we find this difficult? How must we respond?

**11.** Why is it so important that we as Christians also do not lose sight of God's judgment?

## 🙂 getting personal

God has set a day when he will judge the world by the one who always does what is right—Jesus Christ (Romans 2 v 16). God is patient, but there will be an end to his patience because God will give justice in the end.

How much do you share God's passion for justice?

How confident are you that Jesus will judge all people rightly?

How will the day of judgment shape the way you live in this world?

## ⬆ pray

Judgment isn't about God just punching back everybody who has done wrong; it's about God putting right every single injustice.

Use this truth to shape your prayers of praise and confession.

Then ask for God's help to speak his truth to others even when it's costly, just as Elijah did.

# 5 2 Kings 1 v 1 – 2 v 15
# GOING HOME

## The story so far

The Lord is the only God: we cannot serve him alongside anything else, or manipulate him by anything we do, or approach him without a sacrifice for sin.

As God helped Elijah, so we should help people who feel low, both practically and spiritually, pointing them to God's word, people and work, and to Christ.

In this world of injustice, God's people will stand out and suffer, but by trusting in Jesus, our suffering Saviour and perfect Judge, we can keep obeying God.

## ⊕ talkabout

1. What temptations are we likely to experience more as we get older?

## ⊕ investigate

> Read 2 Kings 1 v 1-18

2. In what ways do we see history repeating itself in the events of this chapter?
   • v 2 (compare 1 Kings 16 v 30-33)

   • v 3-4 (compare 1 Kings 17 v 1)

### DICTIONARY

**Moab (v 1):** an enemy country east of Israel, previously subdued by Israel.
**Baal-Zebub (v 2):** false god worshipped by Israel's enemy neighbours, the Philistines.
**Ekron (v 2):** a Philistine city.
**Angel of the Lord (v 15):** a messenger from God.

- v 7-9 (compare 1 Kings 19 v 2)


- v 10, 12 (compare 1 Kings 18 v 38)


- v 15-17 (compare 1 Kings 21 v 17-19)


**3.** In what ways could Elijah be tempted to feel discouraged by Israel? And Ahaziah?


- What should encourage him?


**4.** How would you describe Elijah's attitude in these situations?

# ⊡ apply

**5.** Jesus repeatedly said: "The one who stands firm to the end will be saved" (eg: Matthew 10 v 22). What stops us persevering to the end?

- **Read Hebrews 3 v 12-15.** How can we help each other to persevere in the Christian faith, and what will that look like in practice?

## ⊡ getting personal

As long as your life isn't yet over, don't sit back and think: "I've been a Christian for X years—I've made it; I'm safe." In one sense, we will not be safe until we finally get to eternity—many have shipwrecked their faith. But the God who tells us to stand firm to the end is the One who "will also keep you firm to the end" (1 Corinthians 1 v 8).

Are you sometimes complacent about your final destiny?
Or are you sometimes anxious?
Both are errors. We persevere through God's grace. What will help you keep persevering and also trusting in God's grace?

## ⊡ investigate

### ❯ Read 2 Kings 2 v 1-15

One of the most remarkable things that we discover in chapter 2 is that Elijah and others know that he is about to be taken up into heaven without dying (v 3, 5, 9-10).

**DICTIONARY**

**Elisha (v 1):** Elijah's apprentice.
**Company of the prophets (v 3):** a school for training those who'd preach God's word after Elijah.
**A double portion of your spirit (v 9):** Elisha asks Elijah to treat him like his firstborn son, and so make him his spiritual heir.

### ⊡ explore more

optional

Gilgal, Bethel and Jericho were significant in the history of Israel both for good reasons and bad.

*What great things took place at these sites?*
        *Gilgal (Joshua 4 v 19-23)*
        *Bethel (Genesis 28 v 10-18)*
        *Jericho (Joshua 5 v 13 – 6 v 2)*
*What shameful things were linked with these places?*
        *Gilgal (1 Samuel 13 v 7b-14)*
        *Bethel (1 Kings 12 v 28-33)*
        *Jericho (1 Kings 16 v 34, referring to Joshua 6 v 26)*

*What do you think God's purpose was in taking Elijah on a journey through these places?*

**6.** How does Elijah continue to serve God on his last day on earth?

• What is encouraging about the fact that there are now "companies of prophets" at Bethel and Jericho?

**7.** Look at Elijah's instructions to Elisha (v 2, 4, 6). What is Elijah's purpose in speaking like this to Elisha, do you think?

**8.**   How do we know that Elisha passed the test?

Elijah crossed the Jordan in the same way as Israel on their way into the promised land centuries before (Joshua 3 v 9-17). Elijah's last journey reminds us of the fulfilment of God's promise to his people. Elijah at this point was not so much leaving God's promised land as entering the ultimate promised land of God's eternal kingdom in heaven, which all true followers of the LORD in Israel were longing for (Hebrews 11 v 13-16).

**9.**   What New Testament event is similar to Elijah's exit?

In the Old Testament there aren't many clues about what death is like. It's in the New Testament, where we learn about the death and resurrection of Jesus, that we find out about life beyond the grave.  But Elijah's story gives us one of the few Old Testament glimpses of what death means for God's people.

**10.**  **Read Luke 9 v 28-35.** What does this event show us about the future of God's people after life in this world?

## ⤷ apply

**11.**  Unlike Elijah, God's people today experience physical death. But Jesus Christ has transformed physical death for his followers. In what way will our departure from this world be similar to Elijah's? (Hint: 2 Corinthians 5 v 8 may help you.)

**12.** How will confidence in this future for God's people change the way we live our lives in this world?

## ⊡ getting personal

Christians have even more reasons to be confident about our eternal future than Elijah had. The 19th-century American evangelist, D.L. Moody, once commented: "Some day you will read in the papers that D.L. Moody of East Northfield is dead. Don't you believe a word of it! At that moment I shall be more alive than I am now; I shall have gone up higher, that is all … into a house that is immortal—a body that death cannot touch, that sin cannot taint."

Can you share that confidence? If so, what difference is it making to the way you live in this world?

## ⬆ pray

Take time now to think and pray over things you have learned from these studies.

- Praise and thank your heavenly Father for something you have learned about him.
- Seek forgiveness through Jesus Christ for something about which you have been challenged.
- Ask for the Holy Spirit's help to put into practice one thing you have learned from Elijah's story.

# A man just like us

## Elijah

# LEADER'S GUIDE

# Elijah: Leader's Guide

## INTRODUCTION

Leading a Bible study can be a bit like herding cats—everyone has a different idea of what the passage could be about, and a different line of enquiry that they want to pursue. But a good group leader is more than someone who just referees this kind of discussion. You will want to:

- correctly understand and handle the Bible passage. But also…

- encourage and train the people in your group to do this for themselves. Don't fall into the trap of spoon-feeding people by simply passing on the information in the Leader's Guide. Then…

- make sure that no Bible study is finished without everyone knowing how the passage is relevant for them. What changes do you all need to make in the light of the things you have been learning? And finally…

- encourage the group to turn all that has been learned and discussed into prayer.

Your Bible-study group is unique, and you are likely to know better than anyone the capabilities, backgrounds and circumstances of the people you are leading. That's why we've designed these guides with a number of optional features. If they're a quiet bunch, you might want to spend longer on *talkabout*. If your time is limited, you can choose to skip *explore more*, or get people to look at these questions at home. Can't get enough of Bible study? Well, some studies have optional extra homework projects. As leader, you can adapt and select the material to the needs of your particular group.

So what's in the Leader's Guide?
The main thing that this Leader's Guide will help you to do is to understand the major teaching points in the passage you are studying, and how to apply them. As well as guidance on the questions, the Leader's Guide for each session contains the following important sections:

## THE BIG IDEA

One or two key sentences will give you the main point of the session. This is what you should be aiming to have fixed in people's minds as they leave the Bible study. And it's the point you need to head back toward when the discussion goes off at a tangent.

## SUMMARY

An overview of the passage, including plenty of useful historical background information.

## OPTIONAL EXTRA

Usually this is an introductory activity that ties in with the main theme of the Bible study, and is designed to "break the ice" at the beginning of a session. Or it may be a "homework project" that people can tackle during the week.

So let's take a look at the various different features of a Good Book Guide:

## ⊕ talkabout

Each session kicks off with a discussion question, based on the group's opinions or experiences. It's designed to get people talking and thinking in a general way about the main subject of the Bible study.

## ⬇ investigate

The first thing you and your group need to know is what the Bible passage is about, which is the purpose of these questions. But watch out—people may come up with answers based on their experiences or teaching they have heard in the past, without referring to the passage at all. It's amazing how often we can get through a Bible study without actually looking at the Bible! If you're stuck for an answer, the Leader's Guide contains guidance for questions. These are the answers to direct your group to. This information isn't meant to be read out to people—ideally, you want them to discover these answers from the Bible for themselves. Sometimes there are optional follow-up questions (see ⬇ in guidance on questions) to help you help your group get to the answer.

## ⊕ explore more

These questions generally point people to other relevant parts of the Bible. They are useful for helping your group to see how the passage fits into the "big picture" of the whole Bible. These sections are OPTIONAL—only use them if you have time. Remember that it's better to finish in good time having really grasped one big thing from the passage, than to try and cram everything in.

## ➡ apply

We want to encourage you to spend more time working at application—too often, it is simply tacked on at the end. In the Good Book Guides, apply sections are mixed in with the investigate sections of the study. We hope that people will realize that application is not just an optional extra, but rather, the whole purpose of studying the

Bible. We do Bible study so that our lives can be changed by what we hear from God's word. If you skip the application, the Bible study hasn't achieved its purpose.

These questions draw out practical lessons that we can all learn from the Bible passage. You can review what has been learned so far, and think about practical differences that this should make in our churches and our lives. The group gets the opportunity to talk about what they personally have learned.

## ⊡ getting personal

These can be done at home, but it is well worth allowing a few moments of quiet reflection during the study for each person to think and pray about specific changes they need to make in their own lives. Why not have a time for reporting back at the beginning of the following session, so that everyone can be encouraged and challenged by one another to make application a priority?

## ⬆ pray

In Acts 4 v 25-30 the first Christians quoted Psalm 2 as they prayed in response to the persecution of the apostles by the Jewish religious leaders. Today however, it's not as common for Christians to base prayers on the truths of God's word as it once was. As a result, our prayers tend to be weak, superficial and self-centred rather than bold, visionary and God-centred.

The prayer section is based on what has been learned from the Bible passage. How different our prayer times would be if we were genuinely responding to what God has said to us through his word.

# 1

## 1 Kings 16 v 29 – 17 v 24
# BOOT CAMP

## THE BIG IDEA
The LORD lives and rules; and his power and grace to all people are revealed when, like Elijah, we fear and serve him alone.

## SUMMARY
Elijah lived about 900 years before Christ. Ancient Israel had been divided into two, (see timeline, p6) and King Ahab ruled the northern kingdom, also called Israel. Ahab had disobeyed God by marrying Jezebel, from the pagan nation of Sidon, who brought into Israel worship of the false god Baal. God, it seemed, now only belonged in Israel's history.

There are two parts to this first session— Elijah speaking God's word, and discovering God's ways. First Elijah appears, apparently out of nowhere, to announce a drought sent by God—pitting Baal, supposedly the god of weather and fertility, against the LORD. God proves to be sovereign not only over Israel but the whole world, including Sidon (Jezebel's homeland). Secondly, Elijah is sent on a sort of boot camp, out into the desert alone, and then to Baal's heartland of Sidon to learn surprising lessons about God's purposes, provision, power and grace.

Elijah's story teaches that knowledge and fear of God evaporates the fear of powerful people, helping us speak God's word boldly. We learn why God might send us times of obscurity, isolation and inactivity. And in all this we see that Elijah is only a man like us.

## OPTIONAL EXTRA
1. (To introduce the theme of prophecy and weather) Get people to share proverbs and events that are said to predict weather. Or show an excerpt from the film *Groundhog Day*, where the groundhog makes his weather prediction. (Or google "Groundhog Day in United States" for information about this tradition.) Discuss these "predictions" and why they appeal to people.
2. (To put Elijah into historical context) Conduct a brief survey/quiz that asks (and informs) about Ahab and Jezebel, the history of Israel up to this point, and important events at that time recorded in the Bible.

## GUIDANCE ON QUESTIONS
**1. In what ways do people today think that our modern world has made progress, compared with previous generations?** (People don't have to agree with any examples they give.) Westerners commonly think that today we are more advanced not only in scientific terms, but also morally and ethically. Eg: we believe we are more "liberal" in attitudes towards crime and punishment, personal freedom, sexuality, parenting, other cultures and faiths, etc.; and conversely, less tolerant of racism, sexism, discrimination against the disabled, homosexuals, etc. We tend to regard people of the past as more primitive and less civilised—naïve at best.

- **What do people who think like this often believe about "the idea of God"?** It's thought people used to believe in God because they lacked scientific knowledge; "God" was their only explanation for the mysteries of life. Now, with growing knowledge about our universe, belief in God is apparently no longer needed, but persists in some irrational people because it fulfils an emotional need; better education means belief in God will die out.

**Note:** We'll see that Elijah was also at odds with his culture. He believed that "the LORD, the God of Israel, lives" (17 v 1). Israel had forgotten that. Instead of trusting in this invisible God, Israel believed they needed foreign idol gods.

**2. … What aspect of Ahab's reign is highlighted in chapter 16?** This account mentions only the sins that Ahab committed; specifically his marriage to a foreign, idol-worshipping woman and the idolatry that he promoted in Israel. (See Exodus 34 v 15-16; Deuteronomy 7 v 3-5).

- **Why only this, do you think?** The priority given to Ahab's idolatry reflects God's priority, eg: the first commandment: "You shall have no other gods before me" (Exodus 20 v 3). Because Ahab rebelled against God at this fundamental point, the rest of his legacy is ignored in the Bible.

**3. As [Elijah] speaks [to Ahab], what do we learn about…** Help your group answer the following questions by unpacking Elijah's statement in v 1 (see the italicised words in the quotations below).

- **Elijah's convictions about God?** (1) "As the LORD, the God of Israel, *lives*." God is not a relic of the past, but is powerfully alive, able to act and to overrule any king. (2) "The LORD … *before whom I stand*" (ESV). In Ahab's presence, Elijah is far more aware of standing in the presence of God.
- **Elijah's understanding about himself?** "The LORD … *whom I serve*." Elijah knows that he is God's servant, and his life's mission is to be at God's disposal, willing to go anywhere and do anything (as we'll see), and to say what God has said.

**4. … How could Elijah be so bold?** He is not afraid of Ahab because he is conscious that he stands in the presence of a bigger King, the LORD God Almighty. And his fear of this King evaporates his fear of the lesser king. (See also Isaiah 8 v 13; Matthew 10 v 28; Acts 4 v 18-20.)

- **Read Deuteronomy 11 v 16-17. By what authority could Elijah speak to Ahab like this?** Elijah seemed to know and trust God's promise that if Israel turned away from God to idols, God would withhold rain and bring famine to the land he had given to Israel.
- **When Elijah promises the Baal-worshipping King Ahab that there will be no rain, what spiritual contest does he announce?** Baal was associated with weather (see note in Study Guide after question 2). Elijah's prophecy of drought pits Baal against the LORD. This will reveal who really does control the weather, and so who the true God is.

**5. Read James 5 v 17. What insight does this give us into Elijah's faith and passion?** James says that Elijah prayed for no rain, and it didn't rain for three years. In other words, Elijah initiated a prayer to God based on what he knew from Scripture (eg: Deuteronomy 11 v 16-17), and God answered his prayer. This suggests that Elijah spoke prophetically not so much because God had appointed him as a prophet (there's no mention of that), but because he believed God's words, and he was passionate enough about God's honour to pray that Israel would see the truth of those words. Note the challenge of James' perspective for us: in doing this Elijah was nothing more than a human like us.

**6. APPLY: What is needed for Christians today to be more like Elijah? Think about:**

- **what he confidently knew about God:** He knew that God lives and is sovereign, even when the nation is ruled by ungodly Ahab. We need a deep confidence in God's sovereignty.

- **how he viewed himself:** He knew that he was the Lord's servant—someone who will "go anywhere, do anything" in response to God's word. We need to see ourselves as God's servants, at his disposal.

- **what he prayed for (James 5 v 17):** He prayed in response to what God had already promised in Deuteronomy 11 v 16-17. We need to pray specifically that the people who live around us would see who God is and what he is like, even if that means tough times for us.

**7. Look at verse 3. What is surprising about God's instruction to Elijah?** We would probably want Elijah to stick around at court, and stay in the king's face. But God sends Elijah from a bold and high-profile confrontation with the highest human power in the land straight into obscurity.

**8. What do you think Elijah learns about God in the Kerith Ravine?** He discovers that God provides for us from unexpected sources. He is fed by the ravens—I bet he wasn't expecting that!—and watered by a little brook in the middle of nowhere.

⊗

- **How does Elijah's experience at this point reflect that of Jesus (Matthew 4 v 1-11)?** Both Elijah and Jesus are sent alone into the desert at the beginning of their public ministry. The same pattern is also seen in the lives of Moses (40 years in Midian before returning to Egypt to lead God's people) and David (hiding in the desert and surrounding nations before becoming king).

- **Why do you think God does this?** It seems this is how he equips his servants for what lies ahead, by testing and growing their faith in him. See how even Jesus was equipped for his ministry in this way (Hebrews 2 v 18; 5 v 8-9).

- **What would he learn when the brook dried up?** Never to presume on the grace of God. The God who gives us water can withdraw it. He is under no obligation to ensure that blessing or success continues. Just as he was under no obligation to ensure that Elijah, having confronted Ahab, would stay there in the limelight.

**9. What has been the effect in Sidon of God's word spoken by Elijah in Israel?** The drought promised in Israel has also affected the surrounding areas, like Sidon.

**10. What does God reveal about himself in Sidon, by providing food for Elijah, the widow and her son?** There is no obstacle to God's provision: not the fact that Elijah was far outside of Israel (the land of God's promise and blessing); nor that the woman was a Gentile and probably worshipped Baal; nor the fact that she was of the poorest with no resources of her own to help Elijah. In the very land that was (through Jezebel) the source of Israel's catastrophic sin against God, he reveals both his power and his grace.

- **What does God reveal about himself by raising the widow's son to life again?** He is the only One who can give life—Baal cannot even begin to compete with this! And God gives life, not to someone who deserves it, or who can pay for it, but as an act of grace.

**11. How does the living God compare with Baal?** (1) The famine in Sidon shows that Baal, the local god, is powerless to defend his own people against the living God. Meanwhile, God's power is not confined to the territory of those who worship him. He has complete power over the lives of all people, whether they follow him or not.

(2) The two miracles show how the living God of Israel provides for all kinds of people—here, a "nobody" woman who perhaps has never heard of him and has never worshipped him. The Lord is not like Baal, who would only "bless" those who favour him. Not only does God have power over the lives of all people; he shows grace—undeserved kindness—to all people.

**EXPLORE MORE**
**[From Luke 4 v 16-30] What are the similarities between Israel in Elijah's day and Nazareth in Jesus' day?**
Idolatrous Israel in Elijah's day refused to obey God's word, so he judged the land because of their Baal-worship. In Jesus' day, Israel again refuses to accept the word of God—that Jesus is the Messiah promised by the prophet Isaiah (v 17-21). Though the Jews at first seem impressed with his words, they can't get past the fact that he is the son of the local carpenter (v 22). They aren't really interested in his teaching but only want to see miracles (v 23). When Jesus likens them to Israel in the time of Elijah, they reveal their hearts by trying to lynch him (v 28-29).
**What response from God to Israel's rebellion in the time of Elijah does Jesus highlight here?** God sent Elijah

out of Israel, to a Gentile widow in an idolatrous nation, and there revealed both his power and his grace to all people, by providing her with food and raising her son back to life.
**In Luke 4, what is Jesus saying about himself and the gospel that would be preached in his name?** That since his own people reject him, his gospel and its blessings will be taken to the Gentiles.

**12. APPLY: Think about the experience of Elijah, when God took him out of the limelight and sent him far away into the wilds. What can we learn through such experiences about... • God's priority for our lives?** Sometimes a Christian, for no obvious reason, appears to be set aside and even discarded. We feel inactive, unwanted, even unnoticed. Sometimes God does this so we can learn more about him. To be side-lined, demoted, overlooked, or made redundant may seem so wrong that it shakes our faith. We need to understand that God is far more concerned about his work in us to change our character than our dreams of what he might achieve through us. Chuck Swindoll contrasts how Elijah is described at the beginning of this time of obscurity (merely as "the Tishbite", v 1), and at the end (as a "man of God", v 24). This is how God makes us into people he can use.

• **God's provision?** God sometimes provides for his people from unexpected and unpromising sources—like the wild ravens and the transient Kerith stream, which would dry up every summer. When the "brook" dries up—our health suddenly deteriorates, our job vanishes, our spouse walks out, our fruitful ministry disappears—we can go into freefall as things we took for granted are taken away. It teaches us never to presume on the grace of God. But don't think that God has forgotten you—he hasn't. When the brook dried up, God provided for his servant even more remarkably.

- **God's purposes—in what he does and doesn't give us?** God used Elijah in this obscurity to bring his grace and life-giving power to a Gentile outside of Israel. God can use us in difficult times to bring his gospel of grace and life-giving power into the lives of others, in ways that would not happen if we were still enjoying the good times. You could ask people to share examples of this, either from their own lives or from the lives of other Christians.

# 2 1 Kings 18 v 1-39
# STANDING ALONE

## THE BIG IDEA

We cannot serve the only God alongside anything else, or manipulate him by anything we do, or approach him without a sacrifice for sin.

## SUMMARY

God has responded to Israel's idolatry by sending a three-year drought. Now Elijah announces a public contest between the LORD and Baal on Mount Carmel, to prove that the LORD is the only God. Baal-worship must no longer be accommodated by Israel. They must choose between the living, sovereign true God or the powerless false god. God insists that he alone is to be worshipped and glorified by his people.

The contest reveals the contrasting views of true faith and false religion. False religion uses "magic"—formulas or behaviours that seek to influence a spiritual power. So, when their requests are "ignored", the prophets of Baal escalate their futile attempts to "catch the attention" of their god.

By contrast, Elijah quietly follows God's command. He approaches God by means of a sacrifice for sin. (**Note:** Whatever animal sacrifice meant in Baal-worship, in Israel the purpose of sacrificing a bull as a burnt offering was to make atonement—to make it possible for God to forgive sin; see Leviticus 1 v 3-9.) Then he prays a simple request; he doesn't manipulate God or yell for his attention—he simply listens, obeys, trusts and prays. And God is shown to be everything that Baal is not—supremely powerful beyond any other power, yet attentive to his servant's request.

We are challenged to resist cultural pressure to mix other beliefs with Christian teaching, alerted to the tell-tale signs of false religion's "magic" approach to God, and reminded of the remedy—Christ, the only sufficient sacrifice for our sin, through whom we can wonderfully approach God with confidence.

## OPTIONAL EXTRA

(To set the scene for the contest on Mount Carmel) Get people to list great contests, and perhaps describe their experience of some. Eg: sport—Muhammad Ali vs Joe Frazier in 1975 (the "Thrilla in Manila"), or Isner vs Mahut at Wimbledon 2010

(183 games over 3 days); chess—Karpov vs Kasparov; politics—Blair vs Brown; business—Maxwell vs Murdoch; explorers—Scott vs Amundsen; music—Blur vs Oasis.

## GUIDANCE ON QUESTIONS

**1. Share examples of situations in which you have had to stand alone as a Christian. What helped you to stand firm?** Share stories from personal experience, or the news, or the Bible (eg: Daniel, Paul in 2 Timothy 4 v 16), or history (eg: Athanasius, Luther). Have a couple of examples to get started with. **What was the outcome?** Note that an isolated and courageous stand for the true God won't necessarily result in outright success, as Elijah's example will show (in Session 3).

**2. Why did God choose a drought to show his anger against Israel's worship of Baal, do you think? (Hint: Check out note about Baal on page 8.)** The purpose of Baal-worship was to ensure good weather and fertility in growing crops (see page 8). God responds to Israel's worship of this false weather-god by sending them desperately bad weather that causes famine. Today God still acts like this—through economic instability, or celebrity-idols who "crash and burn", or in any other way that undermines our idols of security and fulfilment.

- **What was the consequence of God's action for his prophet (v 17)?** Ahab calls him: "You troubler of Israel" (probably with expletives edited!). A stand for God does not bring popularity. God's servant must expect unjustified hostility and even blame.

**3. How complete was Israel's rejection of the LORD (V 21)?** Elijah accuses them of wavering between the LORD and Baal. Clearly, the people hadn't abandoned the God of Israel; they'd simply clamped Baal-worship onto their worship of the LORD.

**4. What did Elijah challenge them to do?** Elijah insisted that they had to decide between these two beliefs: to choose one and to reject the other.

- **What was the big thing he wanted them to understand about God?** Elijah was reflecting God's insistence that he alone is to be worshipped and glorified by his people (see Exodus 20 v 3; 34 v 14). God won't have any mixing of his truth with the world's beliefs and ideas. This kind of mix-up always ends in unbelief in the true God.

**5. APPLY: ... Can you think of any examples of [people today mixing Christian teaching with other beliefs]?** Western people are attracted to what they call broad-mindedness. Many still want some sort of Christian heritage, while also buying into other philosophies and religions, taking the bits they like and making a customised belief system. Perhaps your group know of a celebrity or other well-known figure who professes to be a Christian, and yet also speaks out for the practices or philosophy of, say, Buddhism, or some New Age belief. When people say they believe in or follow Jesus, a good question to ask them is: "Which Jesus?" It may be Jesus as the Koran teaches about him, or a Jesus who fits in well with Hindu beliefs, and so not the Jesus of the Bible. Meanwhile, "Christianity" coming from the developing world is often mixed with traditional beliefs and rituals like ancestor worship and witchdoctor magic.

- **Which ideas is it most tempting to combine with Christian teaching in your culture and community?** Think of ways in which this is happening in your local community and even your church. Usually it will be at points where the Christian message seems offensive and divisive, eg: believing Jesus is the only way to God in a community where many follow other faiths.

⊻

• **How should true, Bible-believing Christians respond to these cultural pressures?** See 2 Timothy 4 v 2-5.

**Note:** After reading 1 Kings 18 v 22-29 and the paragraph about Mount Carmel on p15, you could spend a few moments helping your group to imagine some of the details of this dramatic scene.

**6. How did the prophets of Baal try to get the attention of their god? • v 26 (3 things mentioned):** (1) They prepared a sacrifice. (2) They called on the name of Baal. (3) They danced around the altar.

• **v 28:** They slashed themselves with weapons to produce blood.

**7. What was their strategy, do you think?** Their religious approach was to engage in "magic", ie: formulas or behaviours designed to influence a spiritual power to do what you want them to do.

• **What does this show us about their view of Baal and the kind of relationship they had with him?** Baal was not thought of as a personal being with whom his prophets could enjoy a personal relationship; but instead, a powerful force that people could manipulate (perhaps with some difficulty) to achieve their wishes. There was no relationship as such between Baal and his worshippers—they were only seeking to

use his "power" for their own ends.

**8. How did Elijah respond to the Baal-worshippers' attempts to persuade their god to produce fire?** He taunted them. What the NIV politely translates as: "Perhaps he is ... busy" in the original means: "Maybe he is using the toilet!" (cf. ESV). **What was he showing Israel?** His aim here was to humiliate this false god and those who worship him; and so emphasise, by contrast, the majestic sovereignty of the one true God.

**9. What did Elijah do?**

• **v 30:** He rebuilt an old altar of the LORD that had been left to go to rack and ruin.

• **v 31:** He used 12 large stones to build the altar, representing the 12 tribes of Israel (see Exodus 28 v 15-21; Joshua 4 v 1-9), a reminder that Israel was founded by God himself. He dug a trench to hold the water to be poured over the altar.

• **v 32-35:** He drenched the sacrifice with water, filling the trench, to make sure that when the sacrifice was burned up, the onlookers would know for certain that God had done it.

• **v 36-37:** He prayed to the LORD a very simple prayer—a "Declaration of Dependence" on God. There were no magic formulas or frenzies to manipulate God. Elijah knew he could do nothing, and that God needed to do it all.

• **Why did Elijah focus this contest on offering a sacrifice, do you think? (Compare Leviticus 1 v 3-9.)** Discuss why six verses are taken to tell us about Elijah preparing an altar and sacrifice. Remember that God sent the drought to punish Israel for worshipping Baal. Elijah knew that before God would hear or bless Israel, their sin must be dealt with. Whatever animal sacrifice meant in

Baal-worship, the purpose of sacrificing a bull as a burnt offering in Israel was to make atonement—to make it possible for God to forgive sin (Leviticus 1 v 3-9). To ensure his request was heard, Elijah approached God by means of a sacrifice for sin.

**Note:** If people don't know much Old Testament history, it would be helpful to explain Israel's system of animal sacrifices. God's wrath against our sin means that without a suitable, innocent substitute dying in our place, we have no hope of forgiveness, reconciliation with God or blessing from him. This is why God's people in the OT offered up daily animal sacrifices in the Jerusalem temple. (In Elijah's day, however, Jerusalem was in Judah, outside the northern kindom.)

**10. What does this event show us about what God is like?** At God's command (v 36) Elijah makes the test as hard as possible. Then he simply requests: "Answer me, LORD, answer me". And the fire falls. God is seen to be everything that Baal is not—supremely powerful beyond any other power, and yet attentive to the request of his servant, who has approached him exactly as commanded.

• **What does it show us about Elijah's relationship with God?** Elijah doesn't try to manipulate God or yell for his attention. He listens to God and obeys (v 36), trusts God and prays (v 37).

**EXPLORE MORE**
**[John 1 v 29; Matthew 3 v 11-12; Acts 2 v 1-4] How do both the sacrifice and the fire on Mount Carmel preview Jesus Christ? The sacrifice (John 1 v 29):** John the Baptist calls Jesus "the Lamb of God", referring to the Passover (Exodus 12). Lambs were killed and their blood used,

as commanded by God, to save his people from his judgment on Egypt. Later, lambs (and other animals) were sacrificed daily at the tabernacle/temple so that the people's sins could be forgiven and their relationship with God could continue. Jesus is the one that all these sacrifices—the Passover lamb, the animals in the tabernacle/temple and the bull on Mount Carmel—pointed forward to.
**The fire (Matthew 3 v 11-12):** John the Baptist said that Jesus would baptise God's people with the Holy Spirit and fire.
**(Acts 2 v 1-4):** At Pentecost, tongues of fire that rested on the disciples when the Holy Spirit was given to them.
**The fire on Mount Carmel marked the ending of the drought in Israel ... [Acts 2 v 36-41] What did the Spirit's coming mark for God's people at Pentecost?** Assurance that Jesus, though he was crucified, is the King sent by God to save his people (v 36); conviction of sin (v 37); the hope of salvation from sin; forgiveness; the gift of the Spirit; and the possibility of joining God's new people, the church (v 38-41).

**11. APPLY: ... How can we fall into the same mistake [as the prophets of Baal] in approaching God?** By having a checklist of things to do before approaching God. These include: church-going, "quiet times", giving to charity, fasting, religious rituals, being moved in meetings or receiving experiences, making promises, being ministered to by religious celebrities, dressing/speaking in a prescribed way. The longer God takes to answer or the bigger the request, the more extreme we may become in doing these things.

• **What are the tell-tale signs of the "magic" approach to God?**
  • People have no loving and personal relationship with God.
  • They have no confidence before God

because they are never sure that they have done enough to persuade him.

- They become upset with God when he doesn't act as they want, when they have "kept their side of the bargain".
- They don't understand that sin prevents us from approaching God. Or their unresolved guilt makes them fear God.
- When they think they don't need God, they have no interest in him.

**Note:** Returning to the religious or "magic" way to approach God is a constant danger for Christians. It's why the books of Galatians and Colossians were written (see Galatians 3 v 1-5; Colossians 2 v 16-23).

**12. APPLY: Elijah approached the LORD on the basis of a sacrifice for sin and by faith. What does this look like for Christians today?**
Sin brings judgment: it is so serious that something has to die—either the sinner or a substitute. Jesus Christ is the Lamb of God, the one sacrifice that could deal with everyone's sin, once and for all. Jesus took our place, and stood in the line of fire of God's wrath. It was deflected from us onto Jesus on the cross. So Christians come to God through Christ: living for him out of love and gratitude, celebrating what he has done for us on the cross, and praying in his name whenever we come to God.

- **What are the tell-tale signs of this?**
  - Christians are Christ-centred in their speech, motives and teaching. Everything Christians receive depends on him.
  - Christians speak of God as their Father and Jesus as their Lord and Saviour.
  - Christians approach God confidently because Jesus has made that possible. Peace and joy replace guilt and fear.
  - Christians know they are sinners and yet are confident that they are forgiven.
  - Christians can trust God when things do not turn out as they would wish.

# 3 1 Kings 19
# FEELING DOWN

## THE BIG IDEA
As God helped Elijah, so we are to help people who feel down, both practically and spiritually, and point them to our suffering Lord.

## SUMMARY
On Mount Carmel Elijah has seen God answer his prayer with fire. The people have acknowledged that the LORD is the true God. Baal worship has been humiliated and the false prophets destroyed. The three-year drought has been ended. Elijah's expectations are sky-high. Surely there will be a spiritual revival in Israel. Then Jezebel threatens to kill Elijah. Her power is undiminished, whereas Elijah seems abandoned and alone. Elijah plummets into terror and despair, losing perspective, faith in God and the will to live.

So God acts to restore Elijah. This starts with providing for his physical needs—food and rest, a companion and even exercise. But God then goes on to deal with spiritual issues—highlighting Elijah's self-pity, showing himself through his word, sending him back to work, and out to find God's people. Here we see Elijah most clearly to be just like us. None of us—however godly and biblically well-taught—are immune from this kind of weakness of body and mind. God's care for Elijah—tender yet robust, practical and spiritual—shows us how best to love fellow Christians stricken by gloom, depression or despair.

**Note:** This study helps us think about Christians who feel down, including—but not confined to—those suffering from a medically diagnosed depressive illness. Be ready to point people to further help if matters are raised that are beyond your knowledge and expertise; and think about whether anyone in the group might find it difficult to talk personally about this issue.

## OPTIONAL EXTRA

(To help people understand Elijah's feelings here) Read out and discuss an account of depression. Eg: that of the late American writer, William Styron, from his memoir, *Darkness Visible*; an abridged excerpt can be found on www.psychotropical.com (search for "Styron", click on "Depression in Literature" and scroll down). Or see www. desiringgod.org/resource-library (search for "Reflections on the life of William Cowper") for a biographical article about this severely depressive 18th-century Christian poet.

## GUIDANCE FOR QUESTIONS

**1. Can you think of a time in your life when a high point was followed by a low point? How did it affect you?** Many experiences could fit this category: fleeting lows, eg: coming home as a teen from a great party to parents, chores, homework, etc; or more serious episodes of anxiety, discouragement or depression, often caused

by major life-changes that promise much but disappoint us, eg: moving to a new job/area.

**2. Summarise all the things that would have made this point in Elijah's life the pinnacle of his ministry so far.** Elijah has single-handedly represented the true God before a great crowd on Mount Carmel—850 false prophets (1 Kings 18 v 19), King Ahab (see 18 v 41 and 19 v 1), and perhaps over a million people of Israel. He has confronted their idolatry and challenged them to re-commit themselves to the LORD. Elijah's prayer is spectacularly answered (v 36-38). The people acknowledge that the LORD is the true God (v 39). Baal's false prophets are destroyed (v 40). The drought is ended (v 41-45). God empowers Elijah to run 20-plus miles ahead of Ahab's chariot to Jezreel (v 46).

- **What might he expect to happen next, do you think?** Elijah's expectations must be sky-high. Surely the united cry of Israel in v 39: "The LORD—he is God! The LORD—he is God!" is a sign of spiritual revival.

**3. What happens to Elijah next, and how does he respond?** Jezebel threatens to kill Elijah (v 2), to avenge the execution of the false prophets, whom she has personally championed (18 v 19). Elijah reacts in terror—literally running for his life to Beersheba (19 v 3), about 100 miles south of Jezreel.

- **In what way are his expectations disappointed, do you think?** Elijah must have expected a fresh start after Israel's confession: "The LORD—he is God" on Mount Carmel. But chapter 19 opens with Jezebel determined to get revenge on Elijah, her power undiminished. Elijah is vulnerable. No one else steps forward to stand with him against Jezebel. Mount

Carmel, it seems, was an empty victory. **4. What details reveal his state of mind?**
v 4: In Beersheba, Elijah cuts himself off from his one companion, his servant, and heads alone into the desert. There he prays that he might die (v 4), and is then overcome by weariness (v 5). This certainly reads like some of the symptoms of depression—withdrawing from others, suicidal thinking and physical exhaustion.

⊗

• **What do you think of his response? Is it surprising or not?** Both…
**Surprising:** Mount Carmel proved that Jezebel's god is powerless. Who, then, is Jezebel? God alone is worthy of Elijah's fear, which should banish all fear of mere humans. **Unsurprising:** Elijah may have had combat exhaustion—acute anxiety, lack of perspective, abandonment of long-held beliefs and loss of the will to survive. He should have simply laughed at Jezebel. But human bodies and minds are weak. Physical stress often disrupts clear thinking. **Note:** This question can correct two errors. (1) Some people—who perhaps haven't experienced an emotional collapse like Elijah's—think that Christians should never get depressed. (See 2nd Explore More to counter this view.) But Elijah was simply showing humanness— "even as we are" (James 5 v 17). We need to be compassionate to those suffering like Elijah. God was tender with him (Q 5-6). (2) Some people, sympathising with Elijah, resist any idea that he was thinking wrongly and needed gentle correcting. But we need God's truth when we lose God's perspective. We need lovingly to speak gospel truth to those thinking like Elijah here. God was robust with Elijah (Q 7-11).

**5. What are the first actions that God took (v 5b-9) to help his prophet overcome this depressed feeling?**
**v 5b:** God sent him a companion—an angel. (**Note:** "Angel of the Lord", v 7, often indicates a visit of Christ before his incarnation, eg: Genesis 16 v 7, 13.) **v 5, 6:** God gave him sleep. **v 6, 7:** Twice God gave him food, and cooked food at that.
**v 7-8:** The journey from Beersheba to Horeb (about 200 miles) seems to be not just part of Elijah's escape; perhaps God told him to take this journey (see Explore More below). Certainly God approved of it and equipped Elijah for it (v 7). It wasn't very energetic— the pace was about 5 miles a day—but it kept Elijah physically active.

• **What does this show us about God's care for his people?** God is concerned not only for our eternal salvation, but also for our mental and physical wellbeing. "He remembers that we are dust" (Psalm 103 v 13-14). Compare Jesus in Mark: after raising Jairus' daughter, he told her parents to give her something to eat (5 v 35-43). He showed compassion for the crowds listening to his teaching by providing food (6 v 30-44; 8 v 1-8). And after sending his disciples on a mission, Jesus' first concern on their return was that they should get some rest (6 v 30-31).

**EXPLORE MORE**
**What is significant about the place where Elijah ended up? Exodus 3 v 1-15:** At Horeb, Moses first met God at the burning bush, and God revealed his name, and his promises, to his people.
**Exodus 33 v 6 and 18-22:** After leaving Egypt, Israel camped at Horeb (v 6), and God revealed his glory to Moses there. The cleft in the rock (v 22) may be the cave in which Elijah sheltered (1 Kings 19 v 9). It seems that Elijah's arrival at Horeb when he

was so low was part of God's strategy to restore him.

**6. APPLY: What can we learn here about godly ways to approach fellow Christians who are feeling low?** We often assume that knowing God and his gospel should automatically dispel low spirits, leading us to simplistic, and ultimately failing, solutions, which only serve to make someone feel worse.

(1) We must not conclude that depression or discouragement is always caused by outright sin or an evil spirit. Here, Elijah was affected by circumstances—a time of great energy, stress and exhilaration followed by exhaustion, disappointment and danger. Never underestimate the effect of circumstances; none of us are immune from such a reaction, however godly our lives.

**Note:** If people seem unconvinced, look briefly at some Bible characters who expressed both faith in God and deep mental anguish (compare the two passages given). Here are some examples: Job—Job 1 v 20-22 and chapter 3; David—Psalms 11 and 13; Jeremiah—Jeremiah 20 v 11-13 and 14-18; Paul—2 Timothy 4 v 7-8, 17-18 and 9-16.

(2) To focus immediately on looking just for a spiritual solution can make matters worse. At best, some will suggest that simply praying is enough. At worst, someone claiming to have a "deliverance" ministry may inappropriately insist on driving out evil spirits. But God does not say one spiritual thing to Elijah here. Instead, he meets Elijah's needs, providing companionship (an angel), food, rest and exercise. God gives him space for his mood to change, and then deals with the underlying spiritual issues (see questions 7-10).

• **Think of some practical suggestions to help those in low spirits.** People who have experienced depression may be willing to share about what did (and didn't) help them. Suggestions: sending cards or texts; popping round to see them; taking them out for coffee; taking round food so they don't have to cook; offering to do a chore—ironing, mowing the lawn, shopping; taking them away for a break, or paying for them to go away on holiday; keeping them up to date with news if they can't get to church; praying with them (ie: you praying rather than insisting that they pray). **Note:** What is or isn't appropriate depends to some extent on the depth of depression which the person is suffering.

**7. Why does God ask Elijah the question in verses 9 and 13, do you think?** God already knows the answer of course. But he wants Elijah to reflect on what has brought him into the desert, alone, far from the people to whom he has been teaching God's word. (Compare God's question to Adam, Genesis 3 v 8-9.)

• **What does Elijah's answer (v 10 and 14) reveal about his thinking?** He is wallowing in self-pity. So far he has acted on his feelings, rather than in faith and obedience—not trusting God when he heard of Jezebel's threat, but running away (v 3). And he turns the blame on God (v 14). "I have been very zealous for the Lord" (ie: I've done my bit). He sees himself as completely alone: "I am the only one left". His distorted vision sees two of everything—except God. He may feel that God is not near and hasn't kept his word.

**8. In what way does God choose to reveal his presence to Elijah? And what**

**ways does he not choose?** God reveals his presence by speaking to Elijah. Of course God sends the wind, earthquake and fire (also signs of his presence, eg: Exodus 14 v 21; 19 v 18). But it's as if God is saying: *I can send wind, earthquake and fire, but frankly, I have something far more significant that I am going to do.* That "something far more significant" is to speak to Elijah.

• **What is Elijah being taught?** God's presence to comfort, strengthen and restore Elijah comes through his word. On Mount Carmel God's mighty power wowed people and yet they remained unchanged. It's the same for Elijah (see optional extra question below).

⊗

• **Why does God twice ask exactly the same question in verses 9 and 13, and why does Elijah twice give exactly the same reply (v 10, 14)?** This shows that Elijah has not made any progress. The wind, earthquake and fire come and go; Elijah sees the awesome power of God on display, yet he remains stuck in his gloom and self-pity. It's not until God speaks to Elijah (v 15-18) that things change (v 19).

**9. How does God deal with Elijah's perceived isolation?** God knows that Elijah needs fellowship. He links him up with a new friend—Elisha, his heir as God's prophet to Israel (v 16)—and a hidden "church" (v 18). It's Elijah's responsibility to go (v 15, 19); to seek out God's people, rather than wait for them to find him.

**10. What is God's plan for Elijah from this point on?** After all this perhaps Elijah should retire. But God sends him back to work (v 15-17). He's told to anoint Hazael

as king of Syria, Jehu as king of Israel, and Elisha as his own successor. Each play a part in God's plan to bring judgment on Ahab.

**11. APPLY: What can we learn from God's actions about how we further help Christians who are feeling low? Think about the place of the following things:** • **God's word:** God's word is where we encounter God's presence. Many people think God's work in their lives will be like miracles, revivals or the lives of great saints. But God comes to and deals with people through his word. It's unspectacular, but hearing God's word may be the most supernatural thing we will ever experience. So having started to help a low-spirited Christian practically (see question 6 above), we must help them spiritually as well. Share God's word with them and speak it into their situation. Have confidence in God's word: for Christians it is the power of God (1 Corinthians 1 v 18); if we listen to it and do what it says, it brings us freedom and blessing (James 1 v 21-25).

• **God's people:** Like Elijah, we need fellowship. Some people avoid church—perhaps because of spiritual pride, self-centred habit, suspecting insincerity, or fear—and miss out on the strength God wants to give them through his people. God uses his people, gifted by him, to do his work in each of us. See 1 Corinthians 12 v 12-27; Hebrews 10 v 19-25.

• **God's work:** Here the Bible seems to encourage low-spirited people (if not the deeply depressed) to get into some form of gospel work. The 19th-century British preacher Charles Spurgeon believed that if Christians struggling spiritually got involved in looking after poor, needy Christians and telling the gospel to dying people, they would be "mightily restored".

**12. APPLY: What has been your attitude to God's word, God's people and God's work when you have felt down and discouraged?** Many withdraw from these things when despondency and depression strike. As well as giving practical assistance, we must also help them find counsel, support and renewal from God's word, God's people and God's work.

• **What should (and can) your attitude be?** Like Elijah, listen to God's word, seek out his people and obey his call to do his work, whatever that is in our situation.

**EXPLORE MORE**
**What practical help for us has been** provided through Christ's anguish and suffering (Hebrews 4 v 15-16)? Because Jesus suffered and was tempted, he can help us in any weakness (also 2 v 18). When people feel, like Elijah, that their situation is unique; point out that Jesus was tempted in *every* way like us. He understands our temptations to give in to self-pity, give up, run away, want to die, feel abandoned, and doubt God's sovereignty or love. Hebrews 4 v 16 gives the practical help: knowing that Jesus has gone through everything we experience and more, we can "approach God's throne of grace with confidence" to "find grace to help us in our time of need".

# 4 1 Kings 21
# CONFRONTING INJUSTICE

## THE BIG IDEA
In this world God's people suffer; but by trusting in Jesus, our suffering Saviour and perfect Judge, we are able to keep obeying God.

## SUMMARY
In the story of Ahab's lust for Naboth's vineyard, Israel's supposedly most powerful man is reduced by covetousness to behaving like a toddler! Against God's limits on royal power, Jezebel holds that a king can do as he wants, regardless of God's law, justice or the people's wellbeing. She uses slander and judicial murder to secure Ahab's wishes, and the cowardly leaders in Naboth's city collaborate with her.

Naboth, by contrast, is faithful to the LORD. He refuses to win favour with the royal couple by giving up his land, because he knows that it is an inheritance from God, to be kept for his descendants, and for that he dies. Elijah then brings God's verdict against Ahab, just as he is about to move onto Naboth's land. Ahab will not enjoy the fruits of his evil, but he will earn its wages.

Christians today feel pressure from a world where corruption and injustice rule, but where we follow King Jesus, the antithesis of worldly kings—the good Shepherd who has suffered for his people, and the Judge who will impose perfect justice. Like Naboth, we daily face a stark choice between obeying God, or disobeying him in order to get on in the world. And Elijah's faithfulness challenges us to take seriously God's coming judgment and be willing to speak about it today.

## OPTIONAL EXTRA

(To highlight that God gave the land to his people as an inheritance) Ask people to bring in, show photos of, or describe something they have inherited. Or get them to bring in an object they would like to pass on to their children. How much (or little) do they value these things and how important is it to pass them on? For fun, ask them to value the objects (anonymously), based on how much/little they like them, and then have them ranked according to the average "valuation".

## GUIDANCE FOR QUESTIONS

**1. Describe a time when you knew it was right to tell someone something difficult. What excuses came to mind to justify putting off or avoiding this difficult conversation? • If you did go through with it, what helped you to do that?** Have an example of your own to share if needed. Both Naboth and Elijah will have difficult things to say to Ahab. Naboth will die for this. But Elijah too, when he speaks to Ahab, has no good reason to think that he will escape the same fate.

**2. How does King Ahab's request (v 2) sound reasonable?** Ahab offers Naboth a better vineyard, or the going market rate for his land.

**3. [Leviticus 25 v 23; Numbers 36 v 7] What do we learn from God's law about how Israelites were to treat the land? Numbers 36 v 7:** The people must keep the land they have inherited, and not pass it to anyone else—not even another tribe of Israel. **Leviticus 25 v 23:** They mustn't sell the land; they're not owners, but only tenants in the LORD's land.

**• Read Deuteronomy 17 v 18-20. What**

**was expected of the kings of Israel?** The law of Israel limited the king's power. To guard against ignorance of God's law, the king was to write out his own copy and read it throughout his life, so that he would not turn away from God's laws. The king was not to think that he was better than his subjects, or that his rights superseded theirs. **What, then, would have been expected of King Ahab in this situation?** King Ahab should have known from God's law that he was absolutely forbidden to ask Naboth for his vineyard.

**4. Why could Ahab's offer have seemed tempting to Naboth?** (1) Naboth could have a better vineyard or a substantial sum of money. (2) Pleasing the king could mean more access to and influence with Ahab. (3) Displeasing the king could mean a great deal of unpleasantness.

**5. How would you describe Ahab's state of mind over his plans for a vegetable garden?** A small covetous desire had become an uncontrolled obsession. Ahab hides in his palace, face to the wall, pouting like a sulky child (v 4)—simply because he can't get something he wants. Compare Ephesians 2 v 3.

**6. Why does Naboth refuse Ahab's offer?** Naboth knows that God has forbidden his people to give up their "inheritance" (v 3).

**• What motivates him to turn down Ahab, do you think?** Several things: fear of the LORD that overcomes fear even of kings; knowing that the land is not his to sell; trust in God's promises to bless those who obey him (eg: Deuteronomy 30 v 16); concern for his own descendants not to lose the blessing of God's gift to them.

**7. APPLY: Today, how might Christians have to choose between obeying God, or disobeying him in order to get on in the world?** People can share from their own experience or from the news. Have an example ready to use if needed. **Think about the following areas:**

• **the governing authorities:** In many countries Christians come under state pressure to compromise their faith. For more information, see...
www.barnabasfund.org
www.opendoorsuk.org
www.csw.org
Issues include: informing authorities about church leaders, Christian activities and the identity of other Christians; laws against evangelising children and young people, converting people from other religions, distributing Bibles, etc; authorities asking Christians for bribes; or requiring churches to accept state-sponsored leaders only; etc.

• **the workplace:** Bosses sometimes expect staff to lie and cover up; colleagues may dislike Christians working to high standards which could show them up; there may be a strong culture of crude and offensive humour, victimisation, or gossip.

• **the local community:** A community often assumes values that Christians can't subscribe to. Eg: prejudice against minorities; idolising education; treating the police as the enemy; putting career before family; all religions uniting in crises; etc.

• **friends and family:** They may expect Christians to show loyalty to themselves above church, other Christians or Christian ministry, in terms of how Christians use their time and/or money; how they decide where to live or what job to do; how they bring up their children; what they believe and say about controversial issues; etc.

**8. APPLY: Read Acts 4 v 18-31. What do Peter and John teach Christians about how to respond to pressure to disobey God from those in authority?** Obeying God trumps obeying any other authority. We are not to rebel against governing authorities but submit to them. But in Acts 4 we see that allegiance to King Jesus comes first.

• **What do these first Christians teach us about where to find the strength and boldness to do that?** The news about Peter and John spurs the Christians to pray, showing their dependence on God in this situation. They remind themselves of God's past acts and of his word. They put trust in God's power and purposes. Their priority is the honour of Christ's name.

**9. How would you describe Jezebel's view of kingship?** Jezebel believes that Ahab's sulky acceptance of Naboth's refusal is unkingly (v 7). She holds that he should do as he wishes, regardless of God's law, justice or his people's wellbeing; and that she should use any means to help him.

⊗

• **What part did religious rules and laws play in the plot against Naboth?** While disobeying God to get what they want, Ahab and Jezebel follow religious observance and the law when it suits them. Eg: the pretext of a fast (a way of showing repentance!) to gather the community together (v 9); setting up two witnesses against Naboth, in line with Numbers 35 v 30 (v 10); imposing the penalty required by God's law for the crime that Naboth is falsely accused of (Leviticus 24 v 15-16).

• **What does this tell us about rule-keeping?** In itself it's not a sign that an action is right. Sinners love to hide disobedience to God under outward compliance with religious rules. The Bible condemns such cover-ups (eg: Isaiah 1 v 10-17; Mark 7 v 6-13).

## EXPLORE MORE
**At what points did Ahab's kingship and kingdom depart from [God's view of a king and kingdom, Isaiah 32 v 1-8]?**
• The foremost marks of God's king are righteousness and justice (v 1); Ahab and Jezebel did evil and acted with gross injustice against Naboth.
• Godly rulers nurture and protect their people (v 2); Ahab and Jezebel set out to destroy Naboth.
• Under God's ruler, people's eyes and ears are opened to God's truth (v 3) and their thinking and speaking are no longer governed by fear (v 4). Under Ahab and Jezebel the whole nation was deaf and blind to what God says and people feared their power, hence the cowardly collaboration of the community leaders in Jezebel's plot.
• The leaders in God's kingdom are truly noble (v 8), whereas the prominent people in King Ahab's Israel were fools and scoundrels, who were given free reign to do evil (v 5-7). Even Jezebel called Naboth's accusers "scoundrels"! (1 Kings 21 v 10.)
**How is all this fulfilled in the kingdom of Christ?** For each point above, discuss how these things are true of Christ and Christians. Eg: Jesus is God's ultimate king (Luke 1 v 30-33), who came to this world to invite sinful people into his kingdom (Mark 1 v 14-15). He is "our righteousness" (1 Corinthians 1 v 30), and the one chosen by God to judge the world with justice (Acts 17 v 31). Jesus has come as the good shepherd (a picture often used of Israel's kings), who leads, protects and provides for his people, even laying down his life for them (John 10 v 2-4, 11, 14-15). Jesus

opens our eyes to the truth (John 8 v 31-32), and frees his people from fear (Luke 1 v 68-74; Hebrews 2 v 14-15). Those who have been brought into Christ's kingdom through his death will one day serve God by reigning with Christ (Revelation 5 v 9-10); and there all fools and scoundrels will be excluded (21 v 8).

**10. What message for Ahab did God give Elijah at the end of this story?** How God would specifically judge his sin against Naboth. There would be no more opportunities like Mount Carmel, when Ahab could see God's power and acknowledge: "The Lord—he is God". Ahab responded to Elijah's message with meekness (v 27), and received a minor reduction in his sentence (v 29), but there were to be no more opportunities for full repentance before his death (22 v 7). Ask the following question if people are not familiar with what happened to Ahab and Jezebel.

⊗

• **How did the word of the Lord come true?** Ahab: See 1 Kings 22 v 35-38. Jezebel: See 2 Kings 9 v 30-37. Ahab's descendants: See 2 Kings 10 v 1-7.

• **What was Ahab's attitude to Elijah (v 20), and what does it show?** Ahab's words suggest he felt that Elijah was hunting him down. He must know that Elijah is going to say: "This is what the Lord says". When Elijah finally finds him, Ahab bluntly calls Elijah his enemy—which makes God his enemy too.

**11. Look at the timing of the Lord's word to Ahab (v 16-18). Why did God wait until this point, do you think?** Ahab had done all the evil that he needed to do to get the vineyard and he was about to take possession of it. God then intervened through Elijah so that Ahab would not enjoy the fruit of his evil, but he would earn its wages.

☒

• **Why didn't God step in earlier to stop Naboth being killed, do you think?** The Bible has three answers to the question of why God delays justice. You might like to turn to the passages mentioned below to help your group answer this question.
(1) God delays final judgment because of mercy, giving us the opportunity to repent (Romans 2 v 3-4; 2 Peter 3 v 9). It should encourage us to turn to God for mercy and forgiveness.
(2) Delayed justice reveals his wrath against human wickedness (Romans 1 v 18, 24, 26, 28). Counter-intuitively, it is God's kindness that stops us doing what we want, and God's anger that lets us go on as we wish. This should warn us to turn to God for mercy and forgiveness.
(3) Delayed justice shows us that God's judgment is truly just by showing us that sin is truly evil (compare Genesis 15 v 16 and 1 Kings 21 v 25-26). Israel seemed to be blind to Ahab and Jezebel's evil. Although God denounced their idolatry most of all (16 v 31-33; 21 v 26), it seems that wasn't a problem for the people; eg: it wasn't difficult to replace the 850 false prophets executed at Mount Carmel (22 v 6-7). But when sin flourishes, it also worsens. Possibly the slander and murder of a decent man like Naboth would have opened people's eyes to the evil in their midst. When people witness the gross injustice of powerful men like Ahab, they may applaud God's judgment of them.

• **What do you think Ahab's response to God's message shows (v 27-29)— that he was repentant or not? Why? (Skim-reading 22 v 1-28 may help.)**
Two things suggest that this was not true repentance: (1) He didn't restore Naboth's reputation, or Naboth's land to his family; or take any action against Jezebel, the two false witnesses or the cowardly elders of Naboth's city. (2) He continued to consult false prophets, and to revile and try to ignore true prophets of God (see 22 v 1-28). But God eased Ahab's punishment probably to encourage Ahab to keep repenting and seeking mercy from the LORD. However, he squandered his final opportunity.

**12. APPLY: Why is it so important today that Christians continue to teach people about God's judgment?**
Many Christians today feel discomfort with the Bible's teaching about judgment, and under pressure from others—Christians even—to minimise or ignore it. But…
(1) The day of judgment will happen. It's not a myth, a metaphor or a medieval anachronism that's now superseded by science and technology. The proof of this is Jesus' resurrection from the dead (Acts 17 v 31)—which shows that Jesus is without sin, since death could not keep him, and so is uniquely equipped to judge everyone. God is patient, but there is an end to his patience. Ahab's experience shows that.
(2) The day of judgment demonstrates God's justice. God will put right every hurt suffered by every victim. If there is no day of judgment, people can rightly accuse God of being unjust.
(3) The threat of inescapable judgment convinces some people of their need for Jesus Christ to be their Saviour. However much we tell people about Jesus, they will

not turn to him if they do not see their need of a Saviour. Compare the people of Nineveh, who repented and turned to God when Jonah preached coming judgment, and were commended for this by Jesus (Matthew 12 v 41).

- **Why do we find this difficult?** For many reasons. Many people think God's judgment is a big joke. We fear being labelled as throwbacks from medieval times. We don't want to be associated with religious fanatics who use the Bible's teaching on judgment as a cover for preaching hate against people they don't like. Western culture is touchy about anything that judges personal beliefs and lifestyles, so we fear persecution or damaged relationships if we mention judgment. **How must we respond?** By faith in God, his word and his sovereignty

in building his church and reaching the lost. Elijah is an example for us in this. Despite the Israelites' indifference to what happened on Mount Carmel, Jezebel's hatred, Ahab's contempt, and Elijah's own struggles, he continues faithfully to deliver God's word to the king.

**13. APPLY: Why is it so important that we as Christians do not lose sight of God's judgment?** God will vindicate his people and pay back our enemies; this helps us persevere through opposition and suffering (2 Thessalonians 1 v 3-7). Knowing that God is our perfect Judge helps us live motivated by what he sees and thinks, rather than human views and agendas (1 Peter 1 v 17). We must give an account of how we have lived to God; this makes us careful to live in a way that will earn God's commendation (Romans 14 v 10-13).

# 5 2 Kings 1 v 1 – 2 v 15
# GOING HOME

## THE BIG IDEA
Because of Jesus, Christians can, like Elijah, face the end of this life without fear, confident that it is the beginning of life with God in our eternal home.

## SUMMARY
At the end of his story, Elijah has long been in the public eye, viewed as both hero and trouble-maker, subject to pressures that could easily jeopardise the legacy of his life and ministry. Just when ageing might bring more struggles—disappointment, regrets, loss of passion, a desire for rest—Elijah suffers further discouragement. Ahab's

successor again turns to idols; Elijah again has to deliver a message of judgment, and again is persecuted for his faithfulness to God. But Elijah perseveres.

When God announces that Elijah is to leave this world, he simply carries on with his work for that day peacefully and confidently. His journey from Gilgal to the River Jordan replicates in reverse Israel's journey, under Joshua, into the promised land. Elijah is heading to the true, heavenly promised land—his eternal home with God.

We get a glimpse of our future as Elijah leaves this world alive to go up to heaven. It's a preview of how Jesus has transformed death for all of God's people. And it points us to Jesus' ascension, the foundation of our confident hope that Christ will return to gather his people to live with him for ever. We are challenged to persevere to the end, by looking away from present troubles and waiting expectantly for the future that God has promised us.

## OPTIONAL EXTRA

To get people making predictions about possible lasting legacies of famous people (as we consider the end of Elijah's life in this world and the effect of his ministry), hand out a list of famous people who are still alive. Ask people to think of one thing that could be the longest lasting legacy of that person. Suggestions could be humorous or serious. For example: Simon Cowell—a legal ban on high-waisted trousers for men? Bill Gates—polio eradication through the Bill and Melinda Gates Foundation? Or will it be the Windows operating system?!

## GUIDANCE FOR QUESTIONS

**1. What temptations are we likely to experience more as we get older?** There are many answers that can be given here, including: cynicism; disappointment; regret—sometimes unfounded or pointless; loss of enthusiasm for former passions; a desire for comfort over everything else; feeling that we have earned a rest, that younger people should step up to the mark; and so on. Discuss how events in Elijah's life might have tempted him to react in ways like these, and compare how in fact he did respond.

**2. In what ways do we see history repeating itself in the events of this chapter?**
• **v 2 (compare 1 Kings 16 v 30-33):** The new king, Ahaziah, follows in his father's

footsteps by turning to false gods.
• **v 3-4 (compare 1 Kings 17 v 1):** Elijah has to reprise his role as a bringer of God's message of judgment.
• **v 7-9 (compare 1 Kings 19 v 2):** Ahaziah responds as his mother did. Elijah has again earned the enmity of the Israel's ruler. His liberty and probably his life are threatened.
• **v 10, 12 (compare 1 Kings 18 v 38):** God again vindicates his servant by sending fire (twice!), this time to protect Elijah from capture.
• **v 15-17 (compare 1 Kings 21 v 17-19):** Elijah again delivers God's message of judgment directly to the king, and again it comes true.

**3. In what ways could Elijah be tempted to feel discouraged by Israel?** Once again, despite the great victory on Mount Carmel, Elijah witnesses Israel's stubborn idolatry and rebellion against God. Moab, one of the conquered colonies of Israel, who contributed a lot of money to Israel's treasury, has rebelled (v 1). Throughout Israel's history, a decline in power was the sign of God's judgment on his people because of their sin (eg: 1 Kings 11 v 9-14, 23-26). **And Ahaziah?** On the verge of losing his life after an accident, the king tried to enlist the help of foreign gods for his healing. Emphasise how outrageous it was that Ahaziah didn't seek the LORD God. Ahaziah lived in the only nation that had direct communication with the living God. His parents, Ahab and Jezebel, had seen God's power remarkably demonstrated. And Elijah, one of the most prolific miracle-performing Old Testament prophets, was still alive. It was commonly believed then that every nation had its own god, yet Ahaziah didn't even believe that Israel had "its own god"! He knew who Elijah was (v 8) but refused to turn to the LORD, and instead sought out foreign gods; specifically, Baal-zebub—the Philistine god whose name meant "lord of the flies"!

- **What should encourage him?** God again shows that Elijah truly is his servant by sending fire to destroy those who come to capture him (v 10, 12) and by fulfilling the prediction about Ahaziah's death (v 17).

**4. How would you describe Elijah's attitude in these situations?** He is faithful, doing exactly what God tells him, despite any discouragement from Israel's stubbornness, or weariness with bringing yet another message of judgment. Emphasise what a wonderful thing this faithfulness is. Elijah has long been in the public eye, seen as both hero (see 2 Kings 2) and trouble-maker.
**Note:** Both identities could pressure Elijah to jeopardise the legacy of his life and ministry. He has crumbled at one point in a very major way. Yet he continues faithfully to serve and obey God.

**5. APPLY: Jesus repeatedly said: "The one who stands firm to the end will be saved" (eg: Matthew 10 v 22). What stops us persevering to the end?** There are two situations for which Jesus gives his followers the instruction to persevere:
(1) Persecution (Matthew 10 v 22; Mark 13 v 13).
(2) Discouragement and isolation caused by most who claim to be Christians giving up because of increasing wickedness (Matthew 24 v 12-13). We are tempted to give up when our thoughts and feelings are dominated by present troubles and discouragements, leading to a failure to trust in God and his promises.

- **Read Hebrews 3 v 12-15. How can we help each other to persevere in the Christian faith, and what will that look like in practice?** (**Note:** The instruction in Hebrews is also written in the context of suffering; see Hebrews 10 v 32-34.) These instructions are given to "brothers and sisters", ie: the family of believers. In other words, we must help each other—specifically in daily encouragement that challenges our hearts (v 12) and our hearing (v 13, 15)—to take our eyes off our present troubles and instead look confidently to the future that God has promised us. Discuss how your group can get involved in daily encouragement in your church context.

**EXPLORE MORE**
**Gilgal, Bethel and Jericho were significant in the history of Israel both for good reasons and bad. What great things took place at these sites?**
- **Gilgal (Joshua 4 v 19-23):** It was from Gilgal that Israel's pilgrimage in the promised land began. It was where they commemorated the miraculous crossing of the River Jordan.
- **Bethel (Genesis 28 v 10-18):** Bethel was the place where Jacob, while fleeing from his brother, Esau, had a dream of a stairway reaching to heaven, and where God restated the promises that he had made to Abraham. (Later at Bethel, God restated his promises again to Jacob and re-named him Israel, Genesis 35 v 1-15.)
- **Jericho (Joshua 5 v 13 – 6 v 2):** Jericho was the first city in the promised land that was delivered into the hands of the Israelites, not through the fighting skill of Israel but through a mighty act of God.
**What shameful things were linked with these places? • Gilgal (1 Samuel 7b-14):** The first king of Israel, Saul, disobeyed God's

commands about worship there, and so was rejected by God as king.

• **Bethel (1 Kings 12 v 28-33):** After Israel divided into two kingdoms, the northern kingdom established idols, shrines and priests inside their own territory at Bethel, to rival the true worship of the LORD, which could only take place at Jerusalem, inside the southern kingdom.

• **Jericho (1 Kings 16 v 34, referring to Joshua 6 v 26):** As a sign of God's everlasting judgment on the city that had threatened Israel's entry into the promised land, Joshua prophesied a curse on anyone who rebuilt Jericho. Yet an Israelite in the time of Ahab decided to ignore God's word and suffered the consequences.

**What do you think God's purpose was in taking Elijah on a journey through these places?** To remind Elijah from Israel's history of God's sovereignty, covenant love and faithfulness to his promises, all seen again in Elijah's ministry. God's great victory at Jericho was echoed by the outcome on Mount Carmel. Jacob's encounters with God at Bethel, in both the ups and downs of his life, reflected Elijah's own times of triumph and darkness. Gilgal would remind Elijah of the fulfilment of God's promise to give his people a land, and was where Elijah was beginning his final journey to the ultimate "promised land". These places also recalled Israel's rebellion, but the prophets established there highlight God's grace: despite Israel's persistent sin, God continued to speak to them.

**6. How does Elijah continue to serve God on his last day on earth?** Instructed by God (v 2, 4, 6), Elijah journeys from Gilgal to Bethel, then Jericho, and finally to the Jordan River. At each place companies of prophets follow the LORD (they know of God's promise to take Elijah) and look up

to Elijah (they show respect to both Elijah— misguidedly searching for his body, v 16-17—and Elisha, Elijah's successor, v 15.) Probably Elijah set up these groups; now on his last day on earth, he wants to meet these apprentices to counsel, teach and encourage them in the truth, ie: he keeps serving God, just as he has always done.

• **What is encouraging about the fact that there are now "companies of prophets" at Bethel and Jericho?** These were probably "seminaries" for training prophets to preach God's word after Elijah had gone. These sites of past idol-worship and rebellion against God were now places where the word and work of God would continue. Though Israel had not turned wholeheartedly back to the LORD after Mount Carmel, there was hope for the future; Elijah's ministry had not been entirely fruitless.

**7. Look at Elijah's instructions to Elisha (v 2, 4, 6). What is Elijah's purpose in speaking like this to Elisha, do you think?** It seems that Elijah is pushing Elisha away, but actually he is testing him; as if Elijah is asking Elisha: *How committed are you really to this work?* (Compare Jesus' words to would-be disciples in Matthew 8 v 19-22.) Serving God is not mostly about exciting experiences like the Mount Carmel contest, but usually more mundane work, like faithfully teaching God's word to few people. God's servants need perseverance and faithfulness.

**8. How do we know that Elisha passed the test?** Elijah told Elisha that his request (to be Elijah's successor, v 9) would be granted if he saw Elijah taken into heaven (v 10). This is what happened (v 12); Elisha was found to be a worthy successor to Elijah.

**9. What New Testament event is similar to Elijah's exit?** The resurrected Jesus was taken into heaven in a similar way. He had already publicly defeated death; his work on earth was finished and nothing remained to be fulfilled except his final return on the day of judgment. Elijah's exit from this world over 800 years earlier was a tantalising glimpse of future reality—that of death transformed by Jesus through his own death on the cross.

**10. Read Luke 9 v 28-35. What does this event show us about the future of God's people after life in this world?** Elijah's story doesn't end with 2 Kings 2. More than 800 years later, Elijah was still very much alive as he and Moses joined Jesus on the Mount of Transfiguration. He was conscious, able to speak and recognisable. These things were also true of the risen Jesus, and were witnessed on multiple occasions by his disciples. These things are true of all God's people beyond the grave, as 1 Corinthians 15 v 20 makes clear.

⊗

• **What part did Elijah play in the ministry of Jesus here (Luke 9 v 28-35)?** Jesus was about to go to Jerusalem, and the cross (Luke 9 v 51). He was talking about this with Moses and Elijah when Peter, James and John saw him in his glory (v 31). Moses, representing the law, and Elijah, representing the prophets, (ie: the whole OT, which had pointed forward to this mission of Jesus; Luke 24 v 27, 45-47) had come to encourage Jesus as he approached that monumental decision. In life after death, Elijah had an even more significant role than any he had had previously.

**11. APPLY: … In what way will our departure from this world be similar to Elijah's? (Hint: 2 Corinthians 5 v 8 may help you.)** Unlike us, Elijah didn't physically die. But crucially here, Elijah didn't end: he went to be with God. And because of Jesus' death and resurrection, physical death for Christians is simply a transition, like passing through a doorway. The moment we are absent from the body, we are present with the Lord (2 Corinthians 5 v 6-8, NKJV).

**12. APPLY: How will confidence in this future for God's people change the way we live our lives in this world?** Elijah had no fear of leaving this world. He simply, peacefully continued his work. Highlight the connection between Elijah's confidence in his future destiny, and how he lived and worked. Eg: persevering through contempt and hatred because he looked forward to a wonderful eternity. Share ways in which confidence in our eternal future will affect our lives and ministries now, ie: ways in which we can be just like Elijah.

# A selection from the Good Book Guide series...

**1 Peter: Living in the real world**
5 studies. ISBN: 9781904889496

**1 John: How to be sure**
7 studies. ISBN: 9781904889953

**Revelation 2 – 3: A message from Jesus to the church today**
7 studies. ISBN: 9781905564682

## OLD TESTAMENT

**NEW! Judges: The flawed and the flawless** 7 studies.
ISBN: 9781908762887

**Ruth: Poverty and plenty**
4 studies. ISBN: 9781905564910

**1 Kings: The rise and fall of King Solomon** 8 studies.
ISBN: 9781907377976

**Ezekiel: The God of glory**
6 studies. ISBN: 9781904889274

**Jonah: The depths of grace**
6 studies. ISBN: 9781907377433

## TOPICAL

**NEW! Work: Making work work**
8 studies. ISBN: 9781908762894

**Biblical womanhood** 10 studies.
ISBN: 9781904889076

**Man of God** 10 studies.
ISBN: 9781904889977

**Promises kept: Bible overview**
9 studies. ISBN: 9781908317933

**Experiencing God** 6 studies.
ISBN: 9781906334437

**The Holy Spirit** 8 studies.
ISBN: 9781905564217

**Contentment** 6 studies
ISBN: 9781905564668

## NEW TESTAMENT

**Mark 1 – 8: The coming King**
10 studies. ISBN: 9781904889281

**NEW! Romans 1 – 7: The gift of God** 7 studies. ISBN: 9781908762

**Galatians: Gospel matters**
7 studies. ISBN: 9781908762559
(ends 566 in US)

**Ephesians: God's big plan**
10 studies. ISBN: 9781907377099

Visit your friendly neighbourhood website to see the full range, and to download samples
• **UK & Europe:** www.thegoodbook.co.uk • **US:** www.thegoodbook.com
• **Australia:** www.thegoodbook.com.au • **New Zealand:** www.thegoodbook.co.nz •

# thegoodbook
## COMPANY

*Opening up the Bible*

At The Good Book Company, we are dedicated to helping Christians and local churches grow. We believe that God's growth process always starts with hearing clearly what he has said to us through his timeless word—the Bible.

Ever since we opened our doors in 1991, we have been striving to produce resources that honour God in the way the Bible is used. We have grown to become an international provider of user-friendly resources to the Christian community, with believers of all backgrounds and denominations using our Bible studies, books, evangelistic resources, DVD-based courses and training events.

We want to equip ordinary Christians to live for Christ day by day, and churches to grow in their knowledge of God, their love for one another, and the effectiveness of their outreach.

Call us for a discussion of your needs or visit one of our local websites for more information on the resources and services we provide.

UK & Europe: www.thegoodbook.co.uk
North America: www.thegoodbook.com
Australia: www.thegoodbook.com.au
New Zealand: www.thegoodbook.co.nz

UK & Europe: 0333 123 0880
North America: 866 244 2165
Australia: (02) 6100 4211
New Zealand (+64) 3 343 1990

## www.christianityexplored.org

Our partner site is a great place for those exploring the Christian faith, with a clear explanation of the good news, powerful testimonies and answers to difficult questions.

*One life. What's it all about?*